· CREATIVE CRAFTS ·

FUN WITH
PAINT

· MOIRA BUTTERFIELD ·

NOTE TO PARENTS

Some of the paints used for the painting projects in this book, such as acrylic paints and oil paints, don't wash off easily. Turpentine may be needed to wash them off or thin them down. Make sure to supervise when projects use turpentine.

Some projects also use sharp scissors or a craft knife for cutting paper and cardboard. Again, adult supervision is necessary. You may want to use a piece of thick cardboard as a cutting board. Remember to press downwards when using a craft knife.

ACKNOWLEDGMENTS

Paintings made by Brian Robertson,
Katie Scampton, and Anne Sharples
Photographs by David Johnson
Illustrations by Elizabeth Kerr and Joanna Venus

HAMLYN CHILDREN'S BOOKS
Series Editor : Anne Civardi
Series Designer : Anne Sharples
Production Controller : Linda Spillane

First American edition, 1994

Library of Congress Cataloging-in-Publication Data
Butterfield, Moira.
Fun with paint / Moira Butterfield.
p.   cm. — (Creative crafts)
Summary: Includes instructions and "handy hints" for a variety of painting projects, such as straw and splatter painting, stenciling, marbling, and wet paper painting.
ISBN 0-679-83942-3 (trade) — ISBN 0-679-93492-8 (lib. bdg)
1. Handicraft — Juvenile literature. 2 Painting — Technique — Juvenile literature.
[1. Painting — Technique. 2. Handicraft.]
I. Title. II. Series: Creative crafts (New York, N.Y.)
TT160.B96 1993
745.7—dc20   92-18650

Manufactured in Belgium

10 9 8 7 6 5 4 3 2 1

CONTENTS

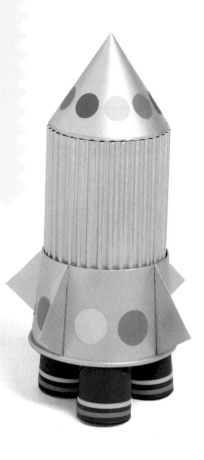

MATERIALS, TIPS, AND HINTS

In this book there are lots of different painting projects for you to try. You can probably find most of the things you need for them around the house, but some may have to be bought from a craft or art supply store. As well as simple step-by-step directions for every project, there are Handy Hints to help you.

For most painting you need poster or tempera paints or watercolors, but a few projects need special kinds of paint, such as acrylics or oils. You will also need fat and thin paintbrushes and special brushes for stenciling.

Poster paint is water-based and washes off easily. It is the cheapest kind of paint to buy.

Powdered poster paint needs to be mixed with water.

Ready-mixed poster paint is sold in jars. You can buy big jars and pour out a little at a time.

You can also buy poster paint in small, hard blocks, which you mix with water.

Oil paints are the most expensive. They come in small tubes and aren't mixed with water.

Brushes, paper, and pots

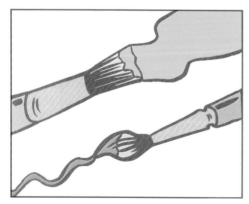

1. Some brushes have flat ends and some have pointed ends. Flat ends are good for painting backgrounds. Pointed brushes are good for painting thin lines.

2. Some brushes have soft bristles and some have much harder, pricklier bristles. It is best to try out different kinds of brushes for different projects.

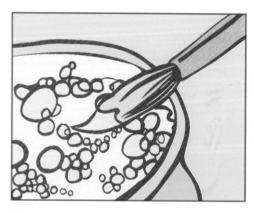

3. Always wash your brushes in soapy water when you have finished using them. Otherwise they will dry stiff, and the bristles will stick together.

Acrylic paints don't wash off easily. They are thick, bright, and usually sold in tubes or plastic jars.

Painting can be a very messy business. It's a good idea to wear an old shirt or apron to keep you clean. Cover your work surface with old newspaper and put a couple of plastic garbage bags on the floor, underneath the table.

It's best to paint in a room where there is a sink close by, so that you can keep changing your paint water.

Keep an eye out for things that might be useful, such as plastic containers, tinfoil, old toothbrushes, cardboard, or old sponges.

Watercolor paints are quite expensive. They come in small tubes or blocks, which are then mixed with water. It is best to use them on white paper.

4. You will need some small cups for water. Old yogurt containers are ideal. An old baking tray makes a very good palette to mix your paints on.

5. If you use paper that is too thin, the paint will make it crinkle up when it dries. Thick watercolor paper is best. It is cheapest if you buy a pad.

6. Strong glue or paste works best on cardboard. Glue sticks are clean and easy to use for gluing lightweight paper.

MIXING COLORS

On these two pages you can find out how to mix paints together to make all sorts of different colors. All you really need are five main colors — yellow, red, blue, black, and white — to make all the colors on the opposite page. Before you start the projects in this book, experiment to see how many colors you can create.

Experiments with color

1. A light color looks brightest against a dark backgound. Try putting white paint on black paper and see how strong the white paint looks.

2. You can make many different shades from one color, depending on how thick or thin the paint is. Try painting a whole picture with just one color.

3. Pastel shades are colors that are mixed with white. Pale pink, pale blue, and pale yellow are all pastel shades. Try making your own pastel colors.

4. When you paint a picture on white paper, leave some of the white showing. It may help to make your painting look fresher and cleaner.

5. Experiment by painting rows of patterns, using two or three colors, as shown. Then you can easily see which colors you like using together best.

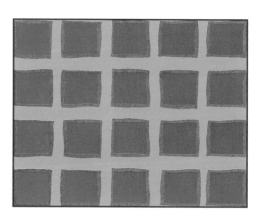

6. Some colors clash with each other, such as red and pink, green or orange. But you can use them together to get a really bright and jazzy effect.

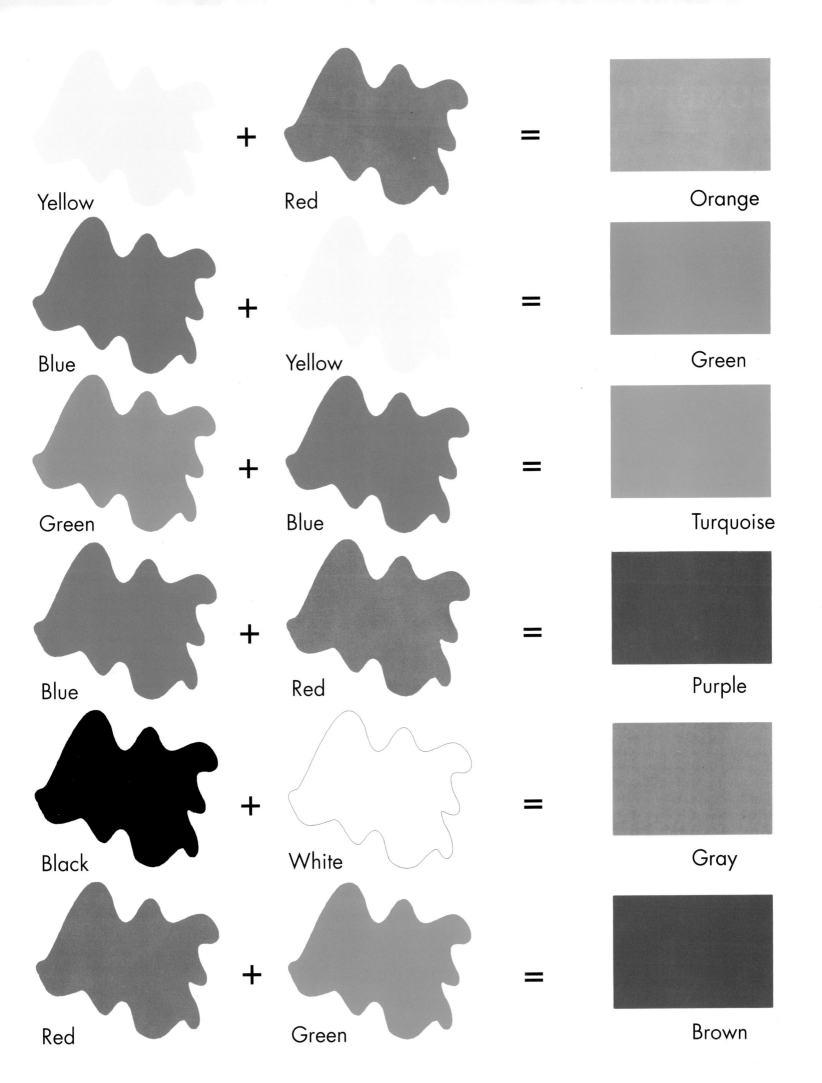

Yellow + Red = Orange

Blue + Yellow = Green

Green + Blue = Turquoise

Blue + Red = Purple

Black + White = Gray

Red + Green = Brown

COMBING AND BRUSHING

You can get all sorts of different patterns and pictures by dragging a comb or a stiff brush across thickly painted paper. Try making your own combs out of thick cardboard, with either blunt teeth or sharp teeth, to use as scrapers.

Things you need

Colored paper
Thin and thick cardboard
Poster paints, including
    gold and silver
Paintbrushes and palette
Plastic comb
Old hairbrush
Crepe paper and
    scissors
Thin ribbon

Draw a coiled-up snake. Paint it and comb patterns in it. Cut out the snake and hang it up.

Golden gift tag

HANDY HINTS

To cover the teeth of a comb or the bristles of a toothbrush with paint, it is easiest to brush the paint on with an ordinary paintbrush.

Try putting blobs of paint onto paper and then dragging it into swirls with a comb.

Golden gift tag

  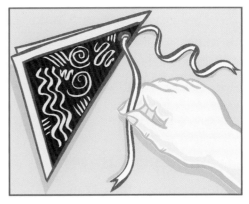

1. Paint a square of paper, about 4 in. by 4 in., with thick, gold poster paint. Make sure the paint covers the paper completely. Leave it to dry.

2. Now paint a layer of black paint on top of the gold paint. While this is wet, run the teeth of a comb across it, pressing down to make different patterns.

3. When the paint is dry, fold the square in half, diagonally. Poke a hole in one corner and thread thin ribbon through it.

Perfect party chains

Perfect party chains

1. Cut two long strips of crepe paper. Cover the teeth of a comb or bristles of a hairbrush with paint. Brush or dot them onto the strips.

2. Let the paint dry, then decorate the other side. When they're dry again, lay the strips at right angles and overlap them, as shown. Tape the ends.

3. Pull out the finished chain to use as a party decoration. You can decorate red and green crepe paper to make perfect Christmas decorations.

STRAW AND SPLATTER PAINTINGS

You can have great fun making all sorts of splotchy paintings using straws, toothbrushes, or nailbrushes. Use colored paper as well as white to make some interesting patterns. It is best to wear an apron and cover the floor or table with newspaper, as this can be a bit messy.

Things you need

Poster paints and palette
Sheets of white and colored paper
Drinking straws, old toothbrush,
  nailbrush, and paintbrushes
Water and newspaper

HANDY HINTS

Practice putting lots of colors together when putting on paint and see the strange effects.

Cut out different cardboard shapes (stencils) and lay them on the paper before you splatter it with paint. They will leave clear shapes on your picture.

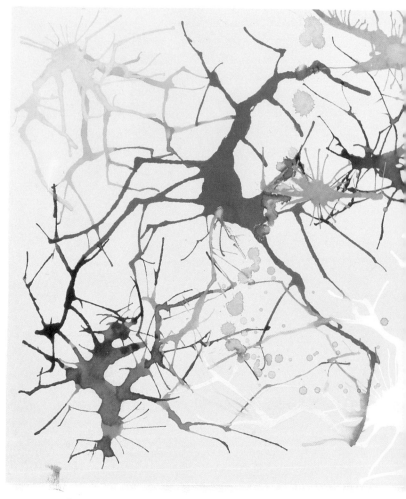

Splotchy straw
painting

Blowing with straws

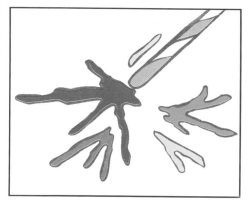

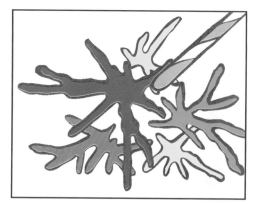

1. Mix your paints with plenty of water to make them runny. Splatter some paint onto your paper with a paintbrush, or paint on runny lines.

2. Blow the runny paint all over the page using a drinking straw. Dab some extra water onto the paper if the paint is not quite runny enough.

3. Gradually splatter on more colors. If you do this while the paint is wet, the different colors will mix together as you blow them around the paper.

Splatter paint through a stencil to make these pictures.

Dab thick paint on paper with the end of a straw to make apple trees.

Lost in space

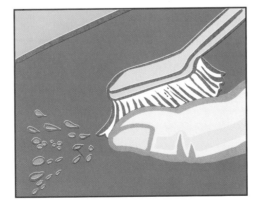

1. To make a starry sky, dab an old toothbrush into white or orange paint. Hold it over a sheet of dark blue or black paper with the bristles facing down.

2. Gently run your finger along the bristles toward you to spray the paint over the paper. (If you do it the other way, you will get sprayed with paint!)

3. Flick paint onto the sky with a paintbrush to make bigger stars. Add a moon, shooting stars, and rockets.

SEEING DOUBLE

The mirror prints on these two pages are quick and easy to make, and every one is different. They are called mirror prints because the pictures on both sides of the folded paper are exactly the same, like the reflection in a mirror. One of the best ways to do them is by using string dipped in paint. The string makes all sorts of swirling patterns on the paper.

Things you need

Sheets of paper, string, and poster paints
Old saucers, paintbrush, and stirrer

Swirling string pictures

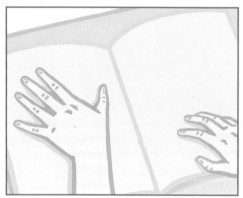

1. Fold a big sheet of white or colored paper in half. Then smooth it out again, as shown.

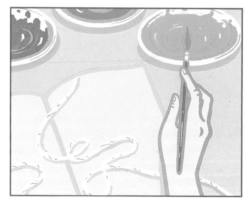

2. Cut two or three short lengths of string. Then put two or three different-colored thick poster paints in old saucers.

3. Stir each piece of string into a different color, as shown. Make sure that they are all completely covered with poster paint.

4. Put the strings down on one side of the paper. Arrange them any way you like, with the ends poking out over one edge.

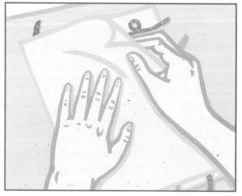

5. Fold the paper in half again on top of the coils of painted string. Then gently smooth it down with your hand, as shown.

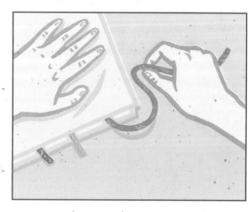

6. Hold the paper down with one hand and pull out the strings, one by one, by the ends. Very carefully unfold the paper.

Paint a person on one side and fold the paper over to make these two terrible twins.

To make two fighting monsters, paint a fierce monster facing the middle. Then fold the paper over.

Paint one half of a butterfly, then fold the paper over.

Paint half a castle and then fold over the paper.

Swirling string picture

13

WAYS WITH WAX

Crayons are made of wax, which is waterproof and does not mix with paint. But if you paint over crayon with one or two layers of thick paint you can make some unusual pictures and patterns. Use lots of crayons and try scratching out a peacock or landscape scene.

Things you need

Crayons
Tempera, poster, or watercolor paints
Thick paintbrush
Thick paper
Small scissors or knitting needle

This beautiful peacock has been scratched through black poster paint.

Wax and scratch

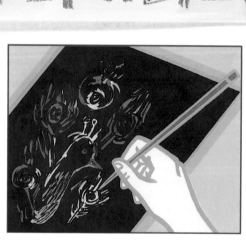

1. Draw thick bands with different-colored crayons on a sheet of paper. Press down hard with the crayons.

2. Paint over the bands of crayon with thick, black poster paint until they are covered with paint. Let the paint dry.

3. Using a knitting needle or scissors, scratch a picture through the paint. The crayon will show through.

HANDY HINTS

Wax shows up best through thinly painted watercolors.

It's easiest to draw your picture first with a pencil. It won't show up when you go over it with crayon.

Use watercolor paint on wax to make patterned picture frames.

Framed wax-on-wax pictures

Wax on wax

1. To make a scratch picture without paint, cover the paper with a light-colored crayon in an oval, as shown.

2. Cover the pale color with a darker one. When you scratch out a picture the pale color will show through.

3. Cut out an oval frame from cardboard for your picture. Decorate the frame with crayons and paint over it with thin paint.

PAINTING WITH ODDS AND ENDS

You don't always need a paintbrush to paint a picture. You can get very strange and interesting effects by dabbing a sponge, cloth, or scrunched-up paper into paint and then pressing it onto paper. Here are some ways to make special paint patterns.

Things you need

Poster paints, old newspaper, and a plate
Tissue paper and empty chip bag
Corrugated paper and waffle-weave dish towel

HANDY HINTS

You can use paper, a sponge, plastic bubble wrap, or a textured cloth to make different paint patterns. Look for things around the house to make your own special paint effects.

When you have practiced making patterns, you can use them to paint interesting pictures and Christmas or birthday cards, like the ones below.

Make cards, gift tags, and pictures out of paintings.

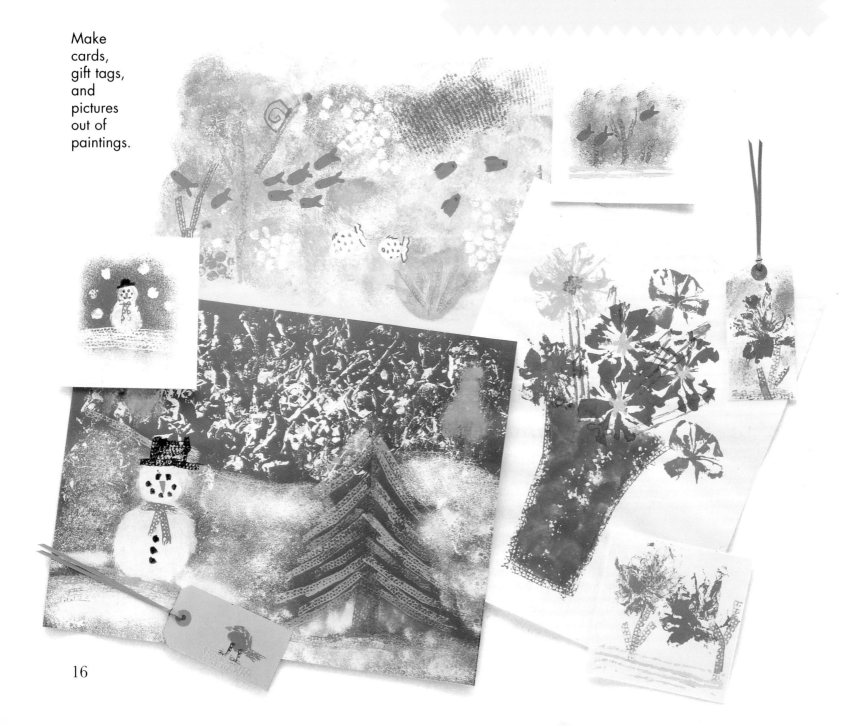

Tissue-paper flowers

1. Cut a circle out of tissue paper. Poke the middle of the circle down between your thumb and forefinger to make a paper rosette, as shown.

2. Mix some poster paint on an old plate. Hold onto the underneath of the rosette, as shown, and dab the top gently into the paint.

3. Press the rosette gently onto a piece of paper. When you lift it up, there will be a flower shape. Do this again or use different-sized circles to make more flowers.

Plastic bag snowstorm

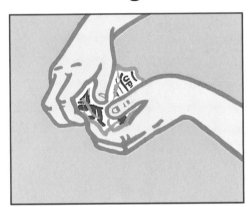  

1. Scrunch up some stiff plastic into a ball. An empty chip bag is best. (A plastic sandwich bag may be too soft.)

2. Mix white poster paint on an old plate. Then dab the ball of scrunched-up plastic gently into the paint.

3. Dab the ball onto a piece of blue paper, as shown, to make a pattern that looks like falling snow.

More patterns to make

For patterned lines, use the edge of a piece of corrugated cardboard.

For a net pattern, use a woven-string dishcloth.

To make swirls, move a scrunched-up ball of paper from side to side.

CARDBOARD CREATIONS

These amazing models are all made with things that you can easily find around the house, such as cardboard tubes, egg cartons, milk cartons, and empty juice cans. Once you have made them, you can paint them with poster paints.

Things you need for the jolly giraffe

5 small cardboard tubes (toilet paper rolls are ideal)
Paper towel roll
Egg carton
Corrugated cardboard
String and strong glue
Tape and scissors
Poster paints

Make a totem pole out of cardboard rolls stuck together and painted. Decorate it with bits of cards.

Make this strange egg carton alien out of an empty egg carton with a cardboard roll mouth and antennae, cardboard tongue, and tinfoil hair.

Jolly giraffe

1. Using strong glue, stick a toilet paper roll onto each corner of the egg carton. These are the giraffe's legs and body. Let the glue dry.

2. To make the neck, cut slits in one end of the paper towel roll and bend them out. Stick the roll onto the egg carton and then tape it down firmly.

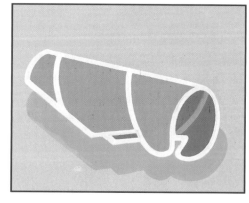

3. For the giraffe's head, cut a toilet paper roll into the shape shown above. Glue it on the neck and tape it firmly in place.

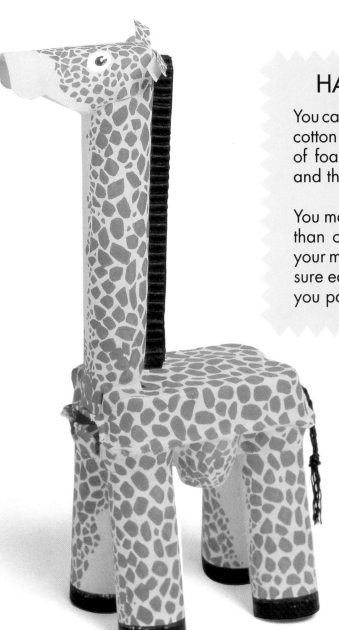

Jolly
giraffe

HANDY HINTS

You can glue things like yarn, cotton balls, foil, and pieces of foam onto your models, and then paint over them.

You may need to paint more than one layer of paint on your model to cover it. Make sure each layer dries before you paint the next one.

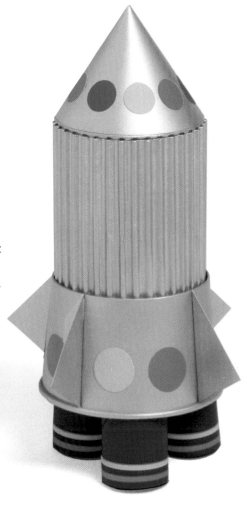

Make this super spaceship out of ice cream containers, toilet paper rolls, and thin cardboard.

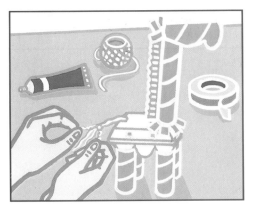

4. For the giraffe's mane, glue a long, thin piece of corrugated cardboard down the back of the neck. Glue on a string tail and fray the end, as shown.

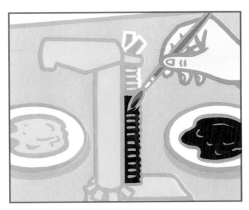

5. Paint the giraffe's body with poster paint. Let it dry and paint on a second coat. Paint the mane and tail. Let them dry.

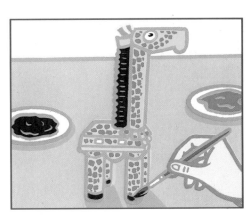

6. When the paint is dry, paint spots all over the giraffe's body. Add eyes and a mouth and hooves, as shown.

19

PAINT PRINTS

You can make striking pictures and wild patterns by printing with leaves, string, vegetables, and even cookies. The secret of making good prints is to use paint that is sticky, not wet. Here are some ideas for printing shapes on paper and fabric.

Things you need

Poster paint
Old tray
Sponge (for a printing pad)
Paintbrush and plain paper
Different-shaped shiny leaves,
  carrots, potatoes, and cookies
Paring knife (Have a parent help.)

Vegetable print writing paper and envelopes

Making a print pad

1. Mix paint with a little water, keeping the paint thick and sticky. Put a sponge inside a tray and pour the paint over the sponge.

2. Press vegetable shapes or leaves onto the sponge to cover them with paint. Then press them onto paper. Rinse out the sponge to change the color.

Vegetable prints

1. Cut a carrot in half. Cut one end, leaving a raised shape, as shown. Cut a different shape out of one end of the other half.

2. Cut a potato in half and pat it dry. Cut one end, leaving a raised shape and use it to print patterns. You can decorate writing paper, envelopes, and fabric.

HANDY HINTS

To print on fabric you need special fabric paints. Make sure you put a sheet of newspaper under your work when you start printing.

If you have put too much paint on your printing shape, dab it on newspaper first to make the paint less thick.

Vegetable print moon and stars

Falling leaves

1. Collect leaves with a shiny, waxy surface that are nice and strong. Brush paint on the leaf or use a printing pad.

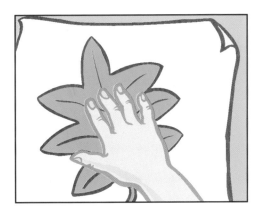

2. Carefully put the painted leaf, facedown, on a piece of plain paper. Press it down gently with your fingers, as shown.

3. Gently peel off the leaf. It will leave a print behind. Make prints with the same leaf in different colors, or try using different leaves.

21

SNAPPY STENCILS

Stenciling makes the same picture or pattern over and over again by painting through (or around) a piece of cardboard. You can stencil on paper, fabric, or wood. It's best to practice with an easy shape when you start. Once you have gotten used to stenciling, try some more interesting and complicated ideas.

Things you need

Stiff cardboard
Watercolor paper
Small scissors or
  craft knife
Thick paint
Stencil brush or
  paintbrush with
  stiff bristles
Natural sponge

HANDY HINTS

Try to paint inward from the outside edge of the stencil hole.

Keep the paint thick. If it's too runny, it will seep underneath the stencil edges and smudge.

You don't always need to dab on an even coat of paint. You can get different textures by letting your brush gradually run out of paint as you dab it on.

Cut-out clown stencil

Cut-out clown

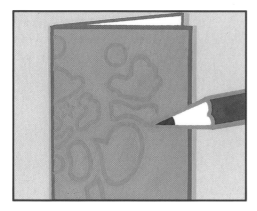

1. Fold a piece of cardboard in half. Draw one half of the clown along the fold line, as shown. Cut around the clown shape and then open the card.

2. Hold the stencil firmly on the paper with one hand. Then dab the paint inside the clown shape, using a special stencil brush.

3. You can use different colors for different parts of the clown. Make sure you allow each color to dry before taking the stencil card away.

Make a border by repeating the stencil pattern many times.

Stencil pattern

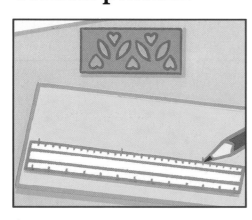

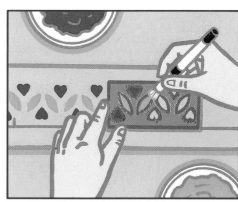

1. Cut out a simple pattern from cardboard about 6 in. long. Draw a straight line on the paper you want to stencil. Make a mark every 6 in. along the line.

2. Put the stencil card on the paper, with the bottom edge of the card running along the line, as shown. This will help keep the pattern straight.

3. Dab paint through the stencil and wait for it to dry. Move the card between the marks, and stencil. Repeat until you have finished.

BEAUTIFUL BUBBLES

Bubble painting is great fun and the patterns you get are always different. You can use bubbles to make pictures or decorate sheets of paper that you can make into many things. You will probably need to practice before you get a perfect bubble painting.

Things you need

Dish-washing liquid
Three or four cup-size
  containers
Lots of straws
Acrylic paints or India inks
Paintbrushes (for mixing)
Watercolor paper

Spider in
a spider's
web

Bubbly book
cover

Bubbly
bookmark

HANDY HINTS

Make sure you are close to a sink. You will need water for the bubble mixtures and for cleaning out containers when you change colors.

It's better to use thick paper because it dries flat.

You can use more than one color on a piece of paper. You don't have to wait for one color to dry before adding another. Bright acrylic paints show up the best.

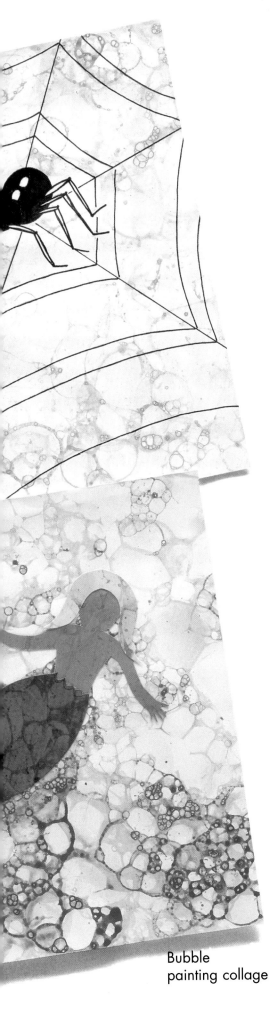

Bubble
painting collage

Blowing bubbles

1. Squeeze about half an inch of dish-washing liquid into a plastic container. Add a spoonful of wet paint or ink and mix.

2. Add a few drops of water. Blow into the mixture with a straw until it bubbles over the edge of the container.

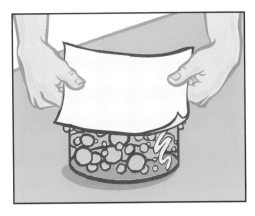

3. Put the paper over the container for a few seconds. When you lift it off you will see a pattern. Cover the paper with patterns.

4. If it doesn't work the first time, experiment with the bubble mixture. Add more water if it doesn't bubble properly.

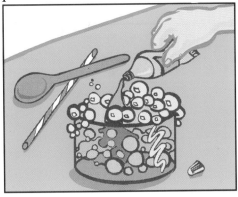

5. If the color is not strong enough to see, add more paint or ink to the bubble mixture, as shown.

6. Lay the finished bubble painting out flat on some newspaper to dry. Make another picture while you are waiting!

MOBILE MAGIC

Here are some ideas on how to make bright and simple mobiles out of cardboard and paint. You may want to choose a theme when you design your mobile, such as this under-the-sea mobile, or this creepy-crawly one.

Things you need

Poster paints or acrylic paints
Thin cardboard, scissors, and
  pencil
Needle and colored thread
Big curtain ring

Under-the-sea
mobile to hang up
in the bathroom

Sea mobile

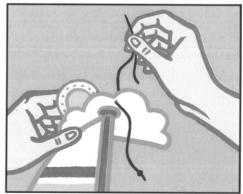

1. Draw a boat shape, as shown, on thin cardboard. Draw nine sea animals or plants.

2. Paint the shapes on one side using different-colored paint. Let the paint dry and cut out the shapes. Now paint the other sides.

3. Thread the needle and knot one end of the thread. Push the needle through the top of the boat and pull the thread until the knot stops it.

For a creepy-crawly mobile, cut out and paint a big sunflower shape. Hang three rows of creepy-crawly creatures from the flower.

HANDY HINTS

Instead of using thread, you can use pieces of yarn. For this you need a needle with a big eye.

You can also hang rows of mobile shapes from a wire or wooden coat hanger that you have painted.

Try different ways to decorate your mobile shapes, such as splattering, sponging, combing, or brushing.

To make a slithery snake mobile, draw a coiled-up snake on some thin cardboard. Cut it out and paint it with poster paints. Push thread through the snake's tail.

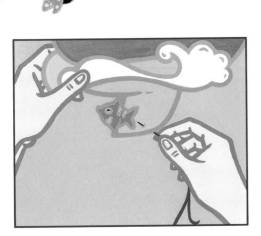

4. Thread the needle again and knot one end of the thread. Push the needle through the bottom center of the boat and pull the thread through, as shown.

5. Push the needle through the top of a sea shape. Cut the thread and tie it in a knot so it hangs down from the boat. Attach another sea shape.

6. Hang three rows of sea shapes from the boat, as shown. Tie a curtain ring to the thread at the top of the boat and hang it on a hook.

PREHISTORIC PAINTING

Prehistoric people were the very first artists. They drew on cave walls using colors made from things like charcoal or soil mixed with water. On these two pages there are ideas for making your own natural paints from things you can find outside, or in the kitchen.

Things you need

Thick paper
Brushes or twigs for painting

Colors you can make

Brown	-	tea/coffee and water
Brown	-	soil and water
Black	-	charcoal
Yellow	-	turmeric
Yellow	-	orange peel
Yellow	-	mustard powder and water
Orange	-	chili powder
Orange	-	carrot
Green	-	grass
Green	-	green pepper juice
Green	-	herbs
Blue	-	cornflower petals
Pink	-	sweet red pepper juice
Red	-	ketchup

Paint a jungle scene and outline it with charcoal.

Natural house and garden

1. For a green grass color, pick a handful of grass. Fold it in half and rub it on a sheet of white paper.

2. To paint the brown parts, mix some water with a little soil from the garden. Different types of soil will make different shades of brown.

3. Collect some blue flower petals for a sky blue color. Wet them slightly and then rub them on the paper so that the color comes off.

HANDY HINTS

Mix tea leaves or coffee with water to get a pale brown-beige color, like old paper.

If you mix colored spice powders, such as paprika, with margarine, the mixture spreads easily and smoothly.

Don't try making paints from berries or fungi of any kind. Some of these are very poisonous. If you do use chili powder, wash your hands well and don't rub your eyes.

Natural house and garden

4. Rub fresh, slightly damp herb leaves, such as parsley or basil, on the paper to get shades of tree green. Your picture will smell of the herbs you use.

5. Mix ground kitchen spices, like chili powder, with soil and water to get yellow and orange colors. Your picture will smell spicy.

6. For another yellow, use a spice called turmeric mixed with water. For pink parts, squeeze the juice out of a red pepper.

PAINTED POTS AND PEBBLES

These colorful flowerpots and pebble paperweights are easy to paint and make good presents. You can decorate many other things with paint as well, such as paper plates, wooden spoons, sticks, driftwood, and shells.

Things you need

Acrylic paints, paintbrushes, and drawing paper
Plate and clear gloss varnish
Terra-cotta flowerpots
Big, flat pebbles

Paint a wooden spoon with one color and decorate to hang in the kitchen.

Pretty painted pot

1. Before you start, decide what to paint on your pot. Draw a design on paper and color it in. Put the flowerpot on an old plate.

2. If you want a background color, paint it on first and let it dry. Then paint your design on top. Use thin brushes for delicate lines and fat ones for bigger patterns.

3. Once the pot is dry, use a thick brush to cover it with a clear gloss varnish. If you want an extra-shiny pot, brush on another coat. Try painting a face or animal on another pot.

Use lots of colors when you paint your pots.

HANDY HINTS

Don't worry if you make a mistake while you are decorating your pots and pebbles. Wait until the paint is dry and then paint over the top.

Put your pot or pebble on a plate to paint it. You can turn the plate around as you paint so that you do not have to touch the wet pot.

Make strange creatures out of painted pebbles.

Paint and varnish paper plates for a wall decoration. But don't eat off them!

Pebble paperweights

1. Before you start, find flat, smooth pebbles or pebbles with interesting shapes. The best place to find pebbles is a stony beach or near a riverbank.

2. Decide what you want your paperweights to look like. You can paint on faces, patterns, and scenes, or make them look like a particular animal, such as a bird, lion, fish, or spooky insect.

3. Paint the pebble all over with a background color, using acrylic paint. Let it dry. Then paint on a face or body, as shown. When the paint is dry, brush on two coats of varnish.

MARBLING MADE EASY

Marbled paper has beautiful patterns, and every sheet looks different. It looks hard to do, but it's really very easy. You can use it as writing paper, for wrapping presents, for covering books, or to make a fabulous fan. Marbling can be messy so you should wear an apron and rubber gloves.

Things you need

Oil-based paints (If you use thick oil paints, you need to thin them with turpentine. Have a grownup help.)
Thick drawing paper and newspaper
Two or three paintbrushes
A shallow baking tray
Vinegar

Marvelous marbled writing set

Strips of marbled paper make good napkin rings.

Marbled gift tags

Marbling paper

1. Make sure that the piece of paper you are going to marble fits into the baking tray. Almost fill the tray with water. Mix in a splash of vinegar.

2. Use a paintbrush to dribble and splatter different-colored paint onto the water. If it's thin enough, the paint will float on top of the water.

3. Use up to four colors. Try swirling them around with a stick, blowing the paint around with a straw, or adding blobs with a brush.

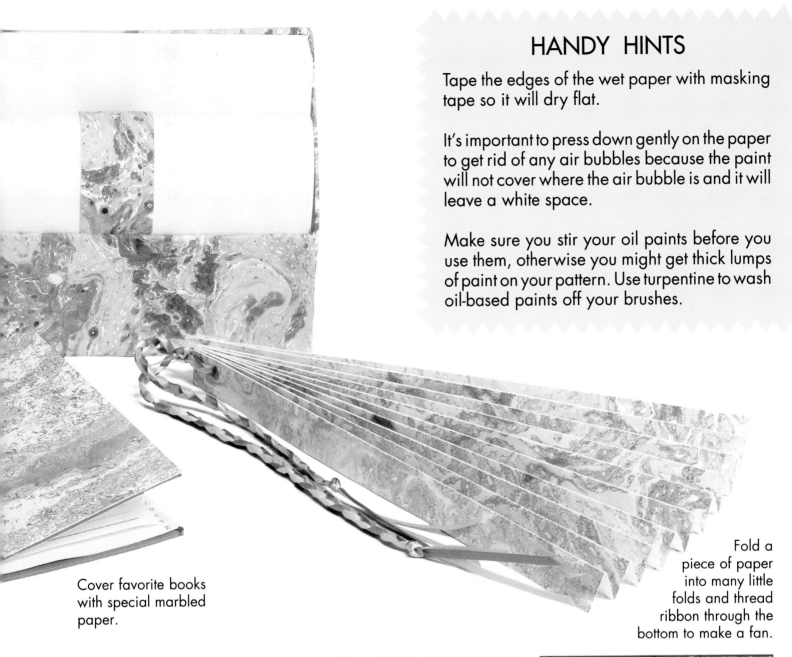

Tape the edges of the wet paper with masking tape so it will dry flat.

It's important to press down gently on the paper to get rid of any air bubbles because the paint will not cover where the air bubble is and it will leave a white space.

Make sure you stir your oil paints before you use them, otherwise you might get thick lumps of paint on your pattern. Use turpentine to wash oil-based paints off your brushes.

Cover favorite books with special marbled paper.

Fold a piece of paper into many little folds and thread ribbon through the bottom to make a fan.

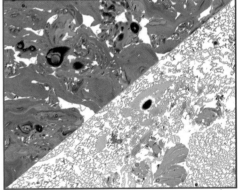

4. Gently put the paper on the top of the water facedown. Tap it very softly with your finger, as shown, to get rid of air bubbles underneath.

5. After a few moments, lift the paper with both hands, holding opposite ends. Let the water drain off the paper into the tray below.

6. Put the paper on newspaper and let it dry. Before you throw the water away, try some more marbling. The pattern will be lighter each time.

WET PAPER PAINTING

You can get all sorts of interesting and exciting effects by painting on wet watercolor paper. It's very useful for making sky and landscape pictures. Try using poster paints, or use watercolors for a more watery look.

Things you need

Paintbrushes and poster paint
Watercolor paper
Container of water

Farmhouse painted on a wash background.

Watery landscape

1. Wet a sheet of watercolor paper by painting all over it with water, as shown. It's best to use a big, fat paintbrush for this.

2. Still using the big brush, paint different colors for the land and sky. The colors will mix together as you paint.

3. When your wash painting is dry, use it as a background for painting plants, buildings, or people.

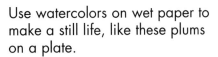

Pale yellow, pink, and blue are good for painting a sunset sky on wet paper.

Use watercolors on wet paper to make a still life, like these plums on a plate.

Using watercolors

1. Sketch the basic shapes of the picture you want to paint, using a very light pencil on dry watercolor paper.

2. Wet a piece of paper. Then use the watercolors to get different effects of light and shade, and dark shadows.

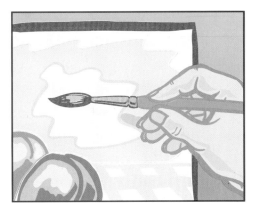

3. If you put one color next to another, they run together. Practice to see what kinds of pictures you can create.

SECRET PAINTINGS

The secret paintings on these two pages change when you want them to. The clever candle pictures are ideal for secret treasure maps, secret letters, and spy messages.

Things you need

White paper
Watercolor or poster paints
White candle
Pencil and paintbrush

HANDY HINTS

If you send a secret picture to a friend, don't forget to send instructions on how to make the picture appear.

It's a good idea to plan out your hidden painting before you start. You can sketch it first and paint over the lines.

This valentine heart is done with a red candle on red paper covered with white paint.

Grinning ghostly painting

Secret candle picture

1. Draw a picture or a secret message on white paper using the tip of a white candle.

2. When you want the picture to appear, paint over it with poster paint or watercolors.

3. The paint will not cover the waterproof wax and the white lines will show through.

Hidden
storm

Secret map
of hidden
treasure

Hidden storm painting

1. Draw and then paint a picture on a rectangular piece of paper. Let the paint dry.

2. Fold over about one-third of the paper. Complete the picture on the blank part, so that it joins the original picture.

3. Make some changes to the things you show on the folded part. When you open the flap, the picture will change.

PAINTING ON GLASS

If you paint a picture on a window it looks like stained glass when light shines through. Poster paints are best to use because they wipe off with water, but you can also use acrylic paints. You can also paint pictures and patterns on jars, glasses, and bottles.

Things you need

Poster or acrylic paints
Palette
Different-size paintbrushes
Ruler

Flowered glass

Birds in a tree bottle and glass

Blooming window box

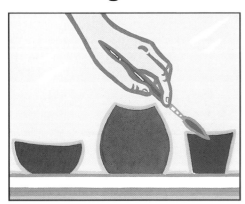

1. Choose a window to paint on. Mix the colors you want to use and paint pots along the bottom of the window. Let them dry, then decorate them.

2. Paint flowers above the pots, either with a brush or by dabbing on wet paint with a scrunched-up tissue, as shown.

3. Paint on stalks and leaves. Paint in flower middles and other small details.

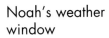

Noah's weather window

Blooming window box

HANDY HINTS

You can make lines and squiggles on the window by scratching gently on the wet paint with the end of a paintbrush.

Use thick paint to avoid drips. If the paint does drip you can wipe it off and start again.

You can buy paints made for painting on glass. Remember to read the instructions and be very careful when you use them.

Super sailing ship

Sweet perfume bottles

Noah's weather window

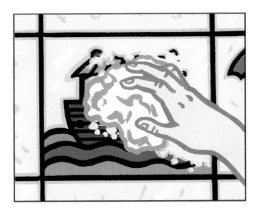

1. Paint nine squares in black paint to look like the black lead in a stained glass window. Run your brush along a ruler edge to get straight lines.

2. Paint a different picture inside each square. Shown here are an ark, weather symbols, an umbrella, and a snowman, but you can paint anything you want.

3. If you want to change the pictures in the future, do the black lines with acrylic paint. They will stay when you wipe off the poster paint pictures.

SILHOUETTE PAINTING

On a dark afternoon, paint a silhouette picture of a friend. Silhouette paintings are dark shadows or outlines painted on a much lighter background. You can also draw around figures cut out from old magazines and then paint in the figure shapes.

Things you need

Paper
Acrylic or thick poster paint
Paintbrushes and palette
Scissors
Cut out figures from old
  magazines or catalogs

Cut out and frame silhouettes of your friends.

Face silhouette

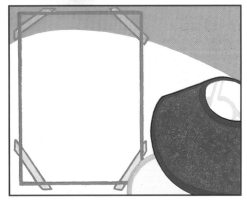

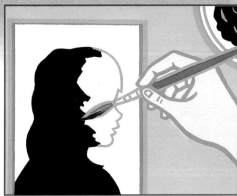

1. Close the curtains or wait until it is dark outside. Switch on a light. Then tape some paper onto the wall at about head height.

2. Ask a friend to stand sideways in front of the paper so that the side of his or her face casts a clear shadow on the paper. Your friend should not be too close.

3. Paint around the outline, or draw around it and paint the line afterwards. Take the paper down and paint in the head shape. Label the silhouette if you like.

40

HANDY HINTS

If you are doing a face silhouette, try moving your friend closer or farther away from the paper. When he or she moves, the silhouette will change shape and size.

You can also paint a person's silhouette just by looking at them from the side, without using a shadow to help you.

You can cut out figures from a magazine, arrange them on some plain paper and paint around the edges with thick paint.

Figure silhouettes

Ask a friend to stand facing left and then right for this double silhouette.

Figure silhouettes

1. Cut out some figures from an old magazine or catalog. Arrange them on top of a sheet of white paper. Leave space around each figure.

2. Hold a figure down while you carefully draw around it with a sharp pencil so you have the outline of a figure. Do the same with the other cutouts.

3. When you have covered the paper with figures, paint inside the outlines. Try using other shapes cut out from old magazines.

41

ARTISTIC ICING

These two pages give you lots of ideas for painting on food, especially cakes and cookies, using white icing and food coloring. You can easily make your own icing or buy it ready-made at the supermarket.

Things you need

White icing (see recipe)
Rolling pin and cookie cutters
Food coloring
Thin paintbrushes and a wooden board
Plate or tray
Plain cookies or cupcakes

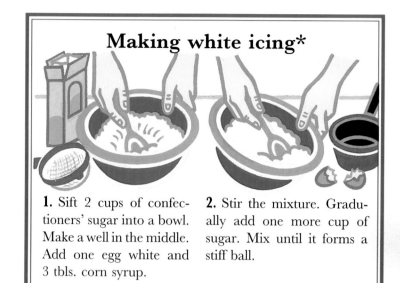

Making white icing*

1. Sift 2 cups of confectioners' sugar into a bowl. Make a well in the middle. Add one egg white and 3 tbls. corn syrup.

2. Stir the mixture. Gradually add one more cup of sugar. Mix until it forms a stiff ball.

Iced and painted cupcakes

Painted cupcakes

1. Use a rolling pin or your hands to press the icing out on a board. Cut circles to fit the cupcakes. Brush the cakes with jam or honey and stick on the icing.

2. Using food coloring, paint a different picture on each iced cake top. You can mix the food colorings together, or add water to make them paler.

3. Before you serve the cakes, put them on a plate or tray in the refrigerator for about 24 hours, or until the paint is completely dry on the icing.

*Ready-made icing may be used if salmonella poisoning is a concern.

Icing
animals

HANDY HINTS

Wrap your icing in plastic wrap and put it in the refrigerator until you are ready to use it. The more you knead it, the softer it becomes.

To roll out icing, lightly butter a cutting board or dust it with confectioners' sugar. With clean hands, knead the icing to soften it. Use your palms to press it out to the thickness you want.

Christmas
decorations

Icing cat

1. Roll some icing into two balls, one larger than the other. Make sure the icing is not too soft. Squash the bigger ball down onto a plate. This is the cat's body.

2. Press the smaller ball onto the cat's body, to make its head. Squeeze around the seam with your finger and a little water to stick the two firmly together.

3. Add some icing ears and a tail, as shown, and then paint the base color. Paint on a face and some whiskers. Put the cat in the refrigerator until it dries.

PHOTO PAINTINGS

Surprise your family and friends with these unusual photo paintings. They are easy to do and make good presents. All you need are photographs, cardboard, and poster paints. You can also make an advent calendar for Christmas using pictures cut out of magazines.

Things you need

Cardboard
Poster paints or watercolors
Strong glue, scissors, and tape
Photographs of your family, friends, or pets
Magazine pictures

Good luck card

Full house card

Full house card

1. Paint a picture of a house, with windows and a door. When the paint is dry, cut the windows and door on three sides to make flaps, as shown.

2. Tape photographs of your family or friends behind the flaps so that when you open the flaps from the front you can see all the faces.

3. Glue the picture to a big sheet of cardboard, as shown.

44

Fashion figures

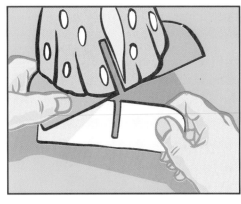

1. Cut the head off a photograph or off a picture of a person in a magazine. Stick the head on a piece of cardboard, as shown.

2. Paint clothes or a silly costume underneath the head. Cut out the whole figure, as well as a rectangular shape at the bottom, as shown.

3. Cut a slit in the middle of the rectangular piece of cardboard. Slide another piece into it to make a stand.

Fold up a strip of paper. Stick a different face onto each fold and decorate the backgrounds.

Fashion figures

HANDY HINTS

For an advent calendar, make 24 windows and a door. Cut out Christmas pictures from magazines to put behind them. Open one window each day until you reach the door on December 25.

SAND AND FLOUR ART

Poster paint mixed with sand or flour makes thick, bumpy paint. It is especially good for painting model scenes, such as landscapes or seascapes. You can also press leaves, twigs, or shells onto the paint before it dries to get an even more realistic scene.

Things you need

Poster paint and paintbrushes
Clean, dry sand
Flour
Cardboard
Plastic knife

HANDY HINTS

It's best to paint on thick paper or cardboard because thin paper is not heavy enough and becomes soggy and wet.

Cut a comb shape from stiff plastic packaging. Then drag it through the paint mixture to make different patterns.

Smiling sandy hippo

Sandy scene

Sandy scene

1. Mix poster paints with sand. Don't make the mixture too thick, or it will stick to your brush and won't spread easily over the paper.

2. Build a picture from the top of the page down. Start with the sky, then paint the middle of the paper, then the bottom.

3. Use a plastic knife to put the mixture on thickly. Try making waves and cuts in it. The tip of a brush is good for making lines and squiggles.

4. Press extra things, such as twigs, leaves, or tinfoil, onto the picture. For more texture, sprinkle sand on top of the wet mixture, as shown.

5. If you add flour and water to the sand mixture, it spreads thinner over a wider area. A mixture of flour and water makes good clouds or snow.

6. Let your picture dry overnight. When it is dry, you can rub some areas with your finger to make them smooth. Shake off any extra sand.